Published by Creative Education
123 South Broad Street, Mankato, Minnesota 56001
Creative Education is an imprint of The Creative Company

Art direction by Rita Marshall
Production design by The Design Lab

Library of Congress Cataloging-in-Publication Data

Franzen, Lenore.
Penguins / by Lenore Franzen.
p. cm. — (Let's investigate)
Summary: Describes the physical characteristics, behavior,
life cycle, habitat, and various groups of penguins, flightless birds
found only south of the equator.
ISBN 1-58341-234-4
1. Penguins—Juvenile literature. [1. Penguins.] I. Title. II. Series.
QL696.S473 F725   2002
598.47—dc21   2001047896

First edition

2 4 6 8 9 7 5 3 1

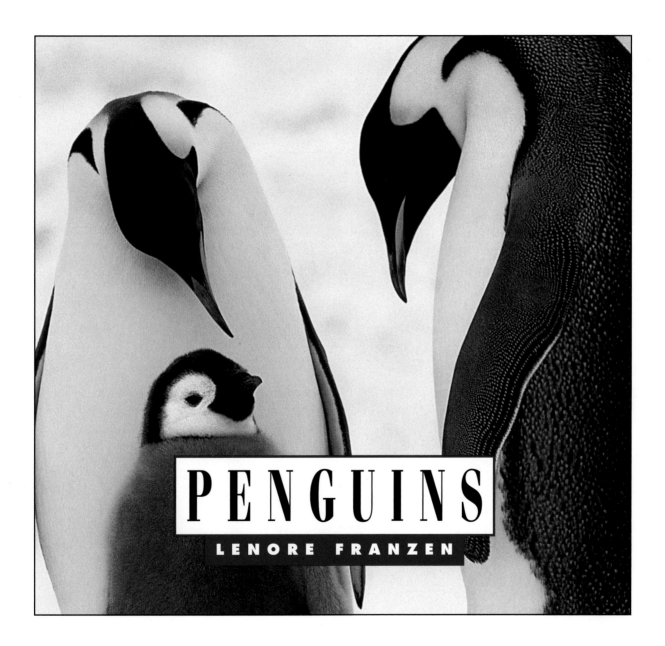

PENGUINS

LENORE FRANZEN

Creative Education

PENGUIN
EXHIBIT

The San Francisco Zoo has a penguin exhibit called Tuxedo Junction that houses 52 Magellanic penguins, the largest colony of this species in captivity.

Their upright waddle and distinctive tuxedo-like coloring make them easy to recognize, yet most penguins live in remote regions of the world. Native only to areas south of the equator, all 17 species belong to the family *Sphenescidae*. Welsh sailors were among the first to sight these unusual-looking birds and named them after the great auk, a flightless seabird that once lived near Newfoundland.

A colony of emperor penguins on the coast of Antarctica

PENGUIN

NUMBERS

*The macaroni is the most abundant of all penguins, with nearly 12 million breeding pairs on the **sub-Antarctic** islands.*

PENGUIN GROUPS

The penguin family is made up of six groups: brush-tailed, crested, banded, large, little blue or fairy, and yellow-eyed. Each group is named for a defining physical trait. Brush-tailed penguins—the Adélie (uh-DAY-lee), chinstrap, and gentoo—have long, stiff, brush-like tails. The five crested penguins—the Fiordland, macaroni, rockhopper, royal, and snares—sport a tuft of gold or orange hair above their eyes. The African, Galápagos, Humboldt, and Magellanic penguins make up the banded group and have a single or double black-and-white stripe across their chests.

Chest stripes identify penguins as members of the banded group

The large group includes the emperor and king penguins. Both have a tear-shaped orange patch on each side of their neck and on their throat. The emperor is the largest of the species, twice the size of the king. While other penguins, on average, stand about 25 inches (64 cm) tall and weigh eight and a half pounds (3.8 kg), the emperor stands about four feet (1.2 m) tall and averages 65 pounds (29 kg).

PENGUIN
FLIPPERS

A penguin's flipper doesn't fold like other birds' wings. The wrist and elbow joints are fused, so only the shoulder joint moves.

The striking markings of an emperor penguin

PENGUIN
SPECIES

The little blue is the only nocturnal penguin. It comes ashore at night to feed its young.

The easily recognized little blue penguin

The smallest penguin species is called the little blue or fairy because of the color of its feathers. Found along the New Zealand and Tasmanian coasts and the southern coast of Australia, the little blue stands a mere 16 inches (41 cm) tall and weighs two and a half pounds (1.1 kg).

The yellow-eyed penguin belongs to its own group. Found in New Zealand, this species has a band of golden feathers around its head. With only about 5,000 left in the world, the yellow-eyed is the most endangered penguin.

PENGUIN

RELATIVES

The penguin's closest relatives are a group of seabirds known as tubenoses, which include the albatross, shearwater, fulmar, and petrel.

Above, small auks, relatives of the penguin Left, the yellow-eyed penguin of New Zealand

PENGUIN

APPETITE

Scientists estimate that five million Adélie penguins eat about 9,900 tons (9,009 t) of krill and small fish every day.

An estimated 250,000 king penguins nest on South Georgia island

LAND AND SEA HOMES

Penguins have adapted to the greatest range of **habitat** of any group of birds. They live only in the **Southern Hemisphere**, from the Galápagos Islands in the **tropics** to the near-freezing waters of the Antarctic Circle. Colonies of penguins are found along the coasts of South America, Africa, Australia, and New Zealand. Antarctica and the many islands nearby are home to seven species, including the Adélie, emperor, and macaroni.

PENGUIN

WALK

Penguins often follow one another in a line when they walk on land. They appear to be playing a game of "follow the leader."

Most penguins actually have two homes. The first is on land or ice, where they come to breed and **molt**. Many penguins live along rocky coastline dotted with low bushes. A few birds nest in grassy areas, forests, or caves. During the winter, the islands near Antarctica are surrounded by **pack ice**, and emperors and Adélies stay on these floating masses to lay their eggs.

King penguins walking single-file

PENGUIN
BREATH

Penguins can hold their breath underwater for a long time. Emperor penguins can stay under for 18 minutes before surfacing for air.

PENGUIN
HEARTBEAT

When penguins dive underwater for food, their heartbeat slows to one-fifth the normal rate, which helps conserve oxygen.

P enguins make their second home in the vast sea. Most spend almost half of each year swimming where the chilly waters encircling Antarctica mix with the warmer waters of the southern Atlantic, Indian, and Pacific Oceans. The ocean currents created there produce a rich food supply. Penguins may spend months swimming in groups, some traveling as far as 2,000 miles (3,220 km) from their breeding area.

Penguins are at home on land or in the water

PENGUIN
NATIVES

Only two penguin species—Adélie and emperor—are native to the Antarctic. The rest live in warmer climates, some as far north as the equator.

Like all penguins, the Humboldt is shaped like a torpedo

CHARACTERISTICS

Penguins are flightless and completely adapted to a life in the ocean. Most birds have hollow bones to make flying easier. Penguins' solid bones add weight and allow the birds to dive for food. Shaped like torpedoes, penguins can swim faster than most people can run. Instead of wings, penguins have powerful flippers that propel them at speeds of up to seven miles (11.3 km) per hour. Penguins swim underwater, surfacing about once a minute for air. Their short legs and webbed feet help steer. When swimming great distances, some penguins **porpoise** out of the water. This technique allows them to more than double their speed. When they reach their destination, penguins launch themselves onto shore with an acrobatic jump of up to six feet (1.8 m).

A penguin swallows fish head-first so the fins don't stick in its throat. Spines on a penguin's tongue and inside its mouth keep fish from slipping or wiggling out.

On land, penguins are less graceful. Their short legs are set far back on their bodies. To keep their balance when walking, these seabirds lean forward and hold out their flippers. Sometimes, waddling over rocks and ice takes too much time and energy, so penguins often plop on their stomachs and toboggan over the snow, using their flippers and sharp claws to propel their bodies forward. Their claws also come in handy for gripping slippery rocks and digging nests.

Above, the spiny mouth of a macaroni penguin Left, gentoo penguins sliding on their bellies

PENGUIN

The smallest penguins are found in the warmest seas, and the largest live year-round in the coldest waters.

PENGUIN

TEMPERATURE

Penguins are warm-blooded, which means their bodies stay the same temperature no matter how warm or cold their surroundings may be.

Penguins are perhaps best known for their black-and-white coloring. This natural camouflage enables them to hide from **predators** and **prey** as they swim. Their black backs blend into the darkness of the water's surface, and from below, their white undersides are hard to see against the light.

Black feathers camouflage penguins on the ocean surface

ach penguin species has markings that set it apart from other penguin species. For example, within the brush-tailed group, Adélies have an all-black head, chinstraps have white across their eyes and a thin black neckband, and gentoos look as if they are wearing a white headband.

PENGUIN
INSULATION

Three marine mammals—the crabeater, Ross, and Weddell seals—have bodies similar to penguins, with layers of fat to keep them warm.

PENGUIN
FLIPPERS

The underside of a penguin's flipper turns pink after swimming because of the increased blood flow to that area.

A chinstrap penguin sporting its telltale neckband

PENGUIN
BEAK

A penguin's diet determines its beak shape. King and emperor penguins have sharp, curved beaks for grasping squid. Rockhopper penguins have short beaks for eating small fish.

Because penguins spend so much time in the sea, they drink a lot of salt water. Special glands above their eyes remove the salt, which then drips out of holes in their beaks. On land, penguins don't see very well. But their eyes are sensitive to blue, green, and violet light, so when they're in the ocean, their vision is sharp and clear.

A gentoo penguin's short beak is ideal for catching small fish

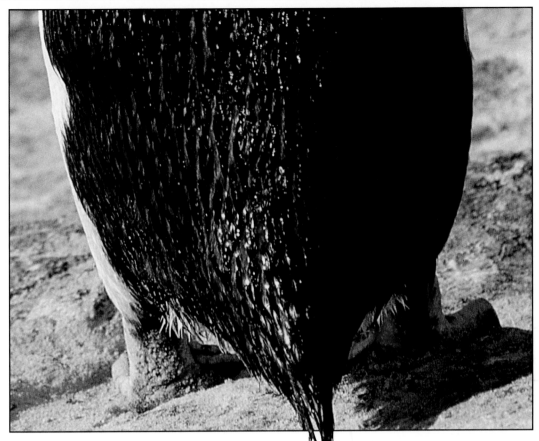

Penguins have insulating feathers and fat, which act like a wet suit and protect the birds from cold air and water temperatures, sharp rocks, and ice. Narrow, straight, and dense, the feathers practically overlap, with more than 70 per square inch (6.5 sq cm). They hold in 80 percent of a penguin's body heat. A layer of **down** close to a penguin's skin adds warmth. Because its feathers provide so much protection, a penguin takes good care of them. When **preening**, a penguin dips its bill into an oil-filled preen gland at the base of its tail, then spreads this special oil over its feathers to waterproof them.

Water slides off a penguin's oiled back and tail feathers

PENGUIN
MOLTING

Unlike all other penguin species, Galápagos penguins molt twice a year instead of once, probably because the hot sun bleaches and damages their feathers faster.

PENGUIN
COOLING

Penguins are so well adapted for cold weather that sometimes they need to cool off. They may fluff up their feathers, pant, or lie down and let heat escape from their feet.

A Humboldt penguin during molting season

Once a year, penguins lose their old feathers and grow new ones in a process called molting. Except for the king penguin, this takes place after breeding. To prepare for molting, penguins first stuff themselves with food to build up fat. The extra energy helps grow new feathers and keeps penguins alive until they can feed again. Without feathers, penguins would not be able to survive the ocean's frigid temperatures when searching for food.

PENGUIN
MEALS

King penguin chicks may eat only three meals during the entire winter. As a result, they may lose up to 68 percent of their body weight before spring.

PENGUIN
MILK

Until the female returns, the male emperor penguin feeds his hungry chick by secreting a kind of milk from the lining of his throat.

An emperor penguin feeding its chick

THE PENGUIN DIET

Penguins are carnivores, or meat-eaters, and feed only in the water. They eat squid, a variety of fish, and krill, a shrimp-like creature that measures about one and a half inches (3.8 cm) long. Penguins dive deep and find most of their food between 32 and 65 feet (9.6–19.5 m) below the surface. After they grab their prey with their sharp beaks, penguins swallow it whole. They store food in a **crop** until they can digest it or feed it to their chicks. Larger penguins consume about five pounds (2.3 kg) of food per day.

PENGUIN
BREEDING

One of the most famous rookeries in the world is located in Punta Tombo, Argentina, where more than one million Magellanic penguins breed.

PENGUIN
CRIES

Even though a penguin rookery may contain hundreds or thousands of hungry, seemingly identical chicks, parents returning with food can distinguish their own by their cries.

A nesting chinstrap penguin calling to its mate

BREEDING CYCLE

Nearly all penguins start breeding in October and November, the beginning of summer in the Southern Hemisphere. They gather in large areas known as **rookeries**. Male penguins perform elaborate courtship displays to define their territories and to attract mates. During these displays, they bow or point their beaks toward the sky, bray loudly, and wave their flippers.

Penguins typically choose mates and nesting sites close to where they were born. Even after months at sea, penguins return to the same place to raise their own young. Scientists believe penguins navigate using the sun, stars, and physical landmarks.

PENGUIN
CALL

The Maori people of New Zealand named the yellow-eyed penguin hoiho, or "noise shouter," because of its loud trilling call.

PENGUIN
NESTS

Penguins on the Galápagos Islands nest in caves, while some snares from New Zealand nest in low tree branches.

Penguins choose mates based largely on appearance

PENGUIN
BREAK

When on land, penguins sometimes rest by leaning back on their heels and supporting themselves with their stout, stiff tails.

O nce paired, a male and female penguin dig out a shallow nest in the ground with their beaks and claws and line it with small rocks, sticks, or grass. After the female lays two eggs, she and the male typically take turns sitting on the nest. Chicks hatch about 40 days later.

Eggs are usually warmed, or incubated, by both parents

Fortunately, penguins have a poor sense of smell. Their droppings create an intense ammonia-like stench at their large nesting sites.

25

Each chick of a medium-size penguin weighs only about three and a half ounces (100 g) when it hatches. It is blind, helpless, and covered with soft, gray down. At first, parents take turns feeding their babies. The adult brings up food from the crop into its mouth. The chick then puts its head inside the parent's mouth to eat. By one month, a chick may weigh four and a half pounds (2 kg). Soon, both parents must hunt so they can bring back enough food for their chicks. While the adults are getting food, the chicks huddle together in large groups for protection against predators.

Above, a nesting site stained with penguin droppings
Left, Adélie chicks

PENGUIN
FOOD

During the day, krill, a penguin favorite, appear as large red patches on the ocean. At night, they shimmer and glow like billions of fire-flies beneath the sea.

A fter a few more months, penguin chicks become **fledglings**. They need all their adult feathers for insulation before they begin to hunt on their own in the cold ocean waters.

An emperor penguin and its fledgling

PENGUIN
BIRTH

The first king penguin chick to hatch outside the Antarctic was at the Edinburgh Zoo in Scotland in 1919. A whaling company supplied the zoo with penguins until 1963.

PENGUIN
PROTECTION

The brood pouch of an emperor penguin works so well that during the middle of winter the egg may be 140 °F (60 °C) warmer than the outside temperature.

Male king penguins warming eggs with their brood pouches

Unlike all other penguins, the emperor and king breed in May and June, during Antarctica's winter. Emperors mate along the Antarctic rim. Kings mate near Cape Horn, South America, and on sub-Antarctic islands, and have the longest breeding cycle of any bird. Also unique to these two seabirds is that they don't build nests. The female lays a single egg on the ice, then the male rolls the egg onto his feet. A **brood pouch** on his lower body keeps the egg warm. While male penguins warm the eggs, female penguins travel to open waters to feed. Male emperors huddle together against the bitterly cold temperatures for up to two months while they wait for their chicks to hatch. During this time, they don't eat and may lose up to 40 percent of their body weight.

PENGUIN
ENEMIES

At Cape Crozier, Antarctica, four leopard seals killed 15,000 Adélie penguins in a 15-week period.

PENGUIN ENEMIES

Scientists have estimated that a medium-size penguin lives about 10 to 15 years, but there are many dangers along the way. A variety of large predators hunt penguins in the ocean, including leopard seals, sea lions, fur seals, and killer whales. On land, penguins have almost no predators, except for large gull-like birds called skuas that steal eggs and young chicks.

Above, a killer whale
Right, a leopard seal

Human activity can also disturb penguin populations. Oil spills damage penguins' feathers so the birds can no longer keep warm. Commercial fishing in areas where penguins feed makes it harder for the birds to find enough food.

PENGUIN
VALUE

In the 19th century, Adélie penguins were slaughtered by the millions for their meat. Also valued was their body fat, which was made into lamp oil.

PENGUIN

EXPRESSION

When the crested rockhopper penguin is disturbed, the black feathers on top of its head stick straight up, and the yellow tufts point out to the sides.

For millions of years, penguins have lived in isolated areas south of the equator. They have divided their time between land and water. This ancient order of seabirds is a fascinating example of how creatures adapt to a wide range of environments in order to survive.

Above, an adult rockhopper penguin
Right, Adélie penguins diving into the sea

Glossary

A **brood pouch** is a loose fold of skin that male emperor and king penguins use to cover and warm an egg until it hatches.

The **crop** is a stretchy throat pouch in which penguins store food until they can digest it or feed it to their young.

Soft, fluffy feathers are called **down**.

When penguin chicks lose their baby down and grow their adult feathers, they are called **fledglings**.

The natural place where an animal makes its home is called its **habitat**.

When birds **molt**, they lose their old feathers and grow new ones.

Huge masses of ice that float on the ocean are called **pack ice**.

To **porpoise** means to leap out of the water at intervals in order to move more quickly.

Predators are animals that hunt and kill other animals.

A bird's act of cleaning its feathers with its beak is called **preening**.

An animal that is hunted or caught for food is considered **prey**.

Rookeries are large breeding grounds where birds gather to pair up, lay their eggs, and raise their chicks.

The **Southern Hemisphere** is the half of the earth that lies south of the equator.

Sub-Antarctic refers to the area surrounding Antarctica where cold polar waters meet the warmer Atlantic, Pacific, and Indian Oceans.

The **tropics** are the hot, humid regions of the earth that lie close to the equator.

Index

beaks, 18, 19
bones, 14
breeding, 22, 23, 27
chicks, 21, 22, 24, 25, 26, 27
coloration, 6, 7, 16, 17, 19

enemies, 28, 29
eyes, 18
feathers, 19, 20
feeding, 10, 15, 19, 21, 26
feet, 14, 15, 19
flippers, 7, 14, 17

group names, 6
homes, 10, 12, 13, 14, 16
nests, 23, 24
penguins
  Adélie, 6, 10, 14, 17, 29

chinstrap, 6, 17
emperor, 7, 13, 14, 18, 27
Galápagos, 6, 20
gentoo, 6, 17
king, 7, 18, 27
little blue, 8

macaroni, 6
Magellanic, 4, 6, 22
rockhopper, 6, 18, 30
yellow-eyed, 8, 23
relatives, 9
size, 7, 8
swimming, 13, 14

Photographs by Peter Arnold (K. Schafer), Robert E. Barber, The Image Finders (Alan Chapman), JLM Visuals (Charlie Crangle, Breck P. Kent), KAC Productions (Peter Gottschling, Greg W. Lasley, John & Gloria Tveten), Tom Myers, Erwin C. "Bud" Nielsen, Root Resources (Mary & Lloyd McCarthy), James P. Rowan, Seapics.com (Bryan & Cherry Alexander, Ingrid Visser)